from

SANDBAR

to

Sophistication

from
SANDBAR
to
Sophistication

The Story of Sunny Isles Beach

Seth H. Bramson

Charleston   London

History
PRESS

Published by The History Press
Charleston, SC 29403
www.historypress.net

Cover image: View of Sunny Isles Beach.

First published 2007

Manufactured in the United Kingdom

ISBN 978.1.59629.201.7

Library of Congress Cataloging-in-Publication Data

Bramson, Seth, 1944-
 From sandbar to sophistication : the story of Sunny Isles Beach / Seth H.
Bramson.
   p. cm.
 ISBN 978-1-59629-201-7 (alk. paper)
 1. Sunny Isles Beach (Fla.)--History--Pictorial works. 2. Sunny Isles
Beach (Fla.)--History. 3. Historic buildings--Florida--Sunny Isles
Beach--Pictorial works. 4. Motels--Florida--Sunny Isles
Beach--History--Pictorial works. 5. Hotels--Florida--Sunny Isles
Beach--History--Pictorial works. 6. Seaside resorts--Florida--Sunny Isles
Beach--History--Pictorial works. 7. Sunny Isles Beach (Fla.)--Buildings,
structures, etc.--Pictorial works. I. Title.
 F319.S96B73 2007
 975.9'38--dc22
                                        2006039551

Sunny Isles Beach Government Center
18070 Collins Avenue, Sunny Isles Beach, FL 33160
305.947.0606 • www.sibfl.net

City Commission

Norman S. Edelcup
Mayor

Roslyn Brezin
Vice Mayor

Gerry Goodman
Commissioner

Danny Iglesias
Commissioner

Lewis J. Thaler
Commissioner

A. John Szerlag
City Manager

Hans Ottinot
City Attorney

Jane A. Hines
City Clerk

Dear Reader,

It is with great anticipation and joy that I present to you our first publication of the 86-year history of Sunny Isles Beach, Florida.

On June 16, 1997, the City became incorporated as a municipality, after a year long effort by its "founding fathers" to achieve city status.

As the second Mayor of this beautiful city, I have been blessed to have been a resident since 1969, and Mayor since 2003. I have seen our community evolve throughout the years, and the many changes are chronicled throughout this book.

Our city has undergone a metamorphosis - from "sandbar to sophistication," and this book certainly reflects our journey through "memory lane" to now, becoming "Florida's Riviera."

It is my hope that you enjoy this book, and enjoy our City!

With warmest regards,

Norman S. Edelcup
Mayor
City of Sunny Isles Beach

With unending amounts of respect and appreciation, this book is dedicated to two people: the late, great Harvey Baker Graves, without whose foresight and dedication to a dream we might not have had Sunny Isles; and Richard C. Schulman, the city's administrative assistant to the mayor and commission and its historian, without whose caring and love for Sunny Isles Beach and dedication to memorializing its great history, we might not have had this book.

Contents

Sunny Isles Beach's "look" is completely different today from what it was in the 1920s: it is a magnificent panorama of high-rise condominiums and hotels, with this view showing north of 167th Street. The sand and surf are still enjoyed by innumerable tourists, residents and their guests. *Photograph by Richard C. Schulman.*

Acknowledgements

The author is indebted to the many people who have helped with the preparation of this book. Unquestionably, the entire Sunny Isles Beach City Commission deserves our gratitude for recognizing the importance of preserving the city's history. This is a sterling feat for a city only ten years old, and I sincerely thank Mayor Norman S. Edelcup, Vice-Mayor Roslyn Brezin and Commissioners Gerry Goodman, Danny Iglesias and Lewis J. Thaler for their enthusiasm in pursuing this project. In addition, our thanks are warmly expressed to the mayor's and commission's aide and city historian, Richard C. Schulman, who did so much to make this project a reality. In addition, the city's director of administration, Alyce Hanson, was always available to provide input and information, and the enthusiastic approval of City Manager John Szerlag is gratefully noted. Harvey W. Graves Jr., Harvey B. Graves's grandson, was totally supportive, as was Susan Lipp, the founder's great-granddaughter. We are most grateful to Susan's dear mother, the late Charlotte Graves Lakeman Patt, who fortuitously preserved many of her grandfather's photos for posterity. Additionally, Ike and Jason Starkman of the Rascal House provided several interesting items for us, while Jackie Biggane, Bill and Penny Valentine and Scott Galvin of the Greater North Miami Historical Society were most gracious in lending me the Sunny Isles material in the society's files. Larry Naukman, director of the Rochester Public Library, and Bob Scheffel, local history division librarian, were extremely helpful in sending needed information. We further acknowledge Sunny Isles Beach Chief of Police Fred Maas; Jeffrey N. Levine; Larry Wiggins; Blair Connor; Ira Giller of the architectural firm of Giller and Giller; Rheta Lastinger; Rose Rice; Kobi Karp, AIA, of Kobi Karp Architects; Arnold Shevlin of R.K. Associates; and Mandy Weightman of the Trump Grande for providing photos and data that assisted us in completing the Sunny Isles Beach story.

Unless otherwise credited, all photographs are from the collection of the author.

Introduction

If the story of Sunny Isles Beach, the city that would officially come to life in 1997, had not occurred, it is unlikely that anybody could have conjured that story up as a work of fiction! It simply does not sound possible that a strip of sand along the beach boulevard—north of what would in 1915 become Miami Beach, separated by a waterway called Haulover Cut and containing a trailer park that would later become part of a county park—could emerge as one of the greatest resort areas of America as well as a beautiful city. Preposterous!

Indeed, it was anything but preposterous, for this incredible tale, this herculean saga of city building, is a story not only of weather and place and beach and buildings but also of people—people with foresight, dedication and determination. Most of these people came from other places, but all of them believed in the future of what at first was little more than a sandbar. This area has become one of the most beautiful and sophisticated cities in America.

Sunny Isles Beach is located across Biscayne Bay and the Intracoastal Waterway from the Miami–Dade County mainland. It faces North Miami, North Miami Beach and the City of Aventura, with the turquoise blue waters of the Atlantic Ocean on the east and the much traveled Atlantic Intracoastal Waterway on the west. The residential city of Golden Beach is immediately to the north, Haulover Park, Haulover Cut and Bal Harbour Village are to the south.

As early as 1912, a cabana was located on the sand strip for the use of bathers. However, our story really begins six years later: in 1918 the man who would found Sunny Isles would enjoy a day's boating trip to the wilds of upper Biscayne Bay, becoming so enthralled with the stunning beauty of the region and its beautiful boating trails that within ten days of that trip he purchased 1,900 acres of canals, river frontage, bays and townsites from the Flagler System's Model Land Company. His family in Rochester, New York, thought that he had lost his mind, but Harvey Baker Graves knew that buying land in south Florida was unquestionably the best investment one could make.

In 1922 work began on what had been named Sunny Isles. By 1925 the first Haulover Bridge—crossing the cut of the same name that connected the Atlantic to Biscayne Bay just north of 102nd Street on the beach side—was completed, allowing those with automobiles to drive along the sandy trail north of Miami Beach. Motoring across the bridge, which was placed at the east edge of the cut, they could enjoy the adventure of a day at Sunny Isles.

Mr. Graves would begin construction of several islands just west of the Ocean Boulevard south of today's 167th Street as well as recreational facilities for those coming over from

Introduction

the mainland, including a bathhouse and casino. A good bit was done prior to the events of 1926 (including the great September 17–18 hurricane) that would be the harbingers of the Great Depression, but for all intents and purposes, after the 1920s Sunny Isles would go into a long state of semi-dormancy.

According to the City of North Miami Beach's website, the state legislature authorized a new charter for the community of Fulford in 1931, on the mainland, allowing incorporation and a name change to North Miami Beach (NMB). Beachfront property was annexed to reflect the 1931 boundaries and to take advantage of the nationwide advertising associated with the Miami Beach area in an effort to capitalize on the city's growing fame. At that time there were about three miles of beach property from Sunny Isles south that were in the incorporated area, so it was a legitimate name.

However, regarding the Sunny Isles area, the City of North Miami website also comments, "Seven miles of Atlantic Oceanfront beachland property from the Broward County line southward to Surfside were removed from the town limits as a result of a 1931 Florida Supreme Court decision. The 1926 hurricane ended plans for a causeway to deliver municipal services to that area of town. With no services being received, the beach area instituted a lengthy court lawsuit to separate and form their own community."

Following the removal of the property from North Miami's jurisdiction, NMB would place approximately three miles of the beach side into its corporate limits. The latter city's annexation ended for the same reasons North Miami's had, and within a few years NMB gave up control of Sunny Isles, whereupon it again became part of unincorporated Dade County.

Sunny Isles developed slowly until following the end of World War II, the only interim event of note being the opening of the fishing pier in 1936. The Howard Johnson's restaurant at 167th and Collins opened circa 1946; the first four-story hotel in Sunny Isles, the Golden Strand, was built in 1946; the Trent Motel opened in 1947; and the first two-story motel in the United States, according to Sunny Isles Beach publicity material, was the Ocean Palm, opening in 1947.

Development accelerated thereafter, and for many years the region's young swains enjoyed not only the beach and Scotty's Drive-In, but also the Rascal House (which opened as Pumpernik's in 1953) and the chance to meet all those gorgeous young women enjoying the fun and sun of motel row.

With the arrival of David Samson, it would all begin to change. Following numerous meetings, the formation of a charter commission and approval by the state and the county, as well as the proposed municipality's voters, the Sunny Isles area would officially come into existence as the City of Sunny Isles Beach on June 16, 1997, with Mr. Samson serving as mayor. In 2007 this stunning and unique community will celebrate its tenth anniversary.

One

Harvey Baker Graves

Harvey Graves was born near Saratoga Springs, New York. His family moved to Rochester, and following school and several years in the printing business, he opened a furniture store there, developing it into one of the largest furniture businesses between New York and Chicago.

Although he came to Florida for the first time in 1905, he would not venture into the Miami area until ten years later. In 1918, as previously noted, Graves would purchase 1,900 acres, including more than nine miles of Biscayne Bay, Biscayne and Oleta Rivers and Dumfoundling Bay water frontage, along with Bella Vista. The following year he built his winter home at Fallasen Park, in Miami's Lemon City subdivision. In 1924 and 1925, the Sunny Isles Water Company's plant was completed at a cost of over $100,000. Mr. Graves began the filling of several islands, just west of the Ocean Boulevard (today's Collins Avenue) and south of today's 167th Street, which is simply the continuation of Northeast 163rd Street from the Miami side.

In constructing Sunny Isles, Mr. Graves referred to it as "a place in the sun on the ocean." The original Graves property (known for many years as the Graves Tract, though few people knew why it was called that) extended west to today's U.S. Highway 1 and included land both north and south of Northeast 163rd Street on the mainland side.

Among the islands that were filled and named were Fairyland Island, the recreation island, Atlantic Island and Poinciana Island, both planned for residential use. A major bathhouse and casino, which existed through the Depression and into the World War II years, was built at Sunny Isles Beach Boulevard and the ocean, but with the catastrophic events of 1926, business in Miami and the surrounding area began to decline precipitously.

Mr. Graves was active in northeast Dade County until 1935, when he donated 56 acres to the county to complement the 105 acres that A.O. Greynolds gave to complete Greynolds Park. Shortly thereafter, Graves would return to Rochester, his long, active and marvelously productive life in both central New York and southern Florida coming to an end in 1936. He was almost eighty-one years old.

Harvey Baker Graves (May 6, 1855–January 14, 1936). It was he who would begin the work of building what would eventually become a famous city along the ocean north of Miami Beach. Graves's holdings once included much of North Miami Beach east of Biscayne Boulevard, known as the Graves Tract, upon which the Biscayne Bay Campus of Florida International University was built. Biscayne Landings, a multi-use development, is currently under construction. *Courtesy Harvey W. Graves Jr.*

On February 1, 1901, four years before his first trip to Florida, Harvey B. Graves and his family posed for this striking portrait. (From left) Mrs. Charlotte Graves; baby Ruth on her lap; Emma, twelve; Harvey Baker Graves; Harvey Wilbur Graves, fourteen; Charlotte, eight; and Frances, five. *Courtesy collection of Susan Lipp.*

Harvey Baker Graves

Above and below: In 1919, the year after he purchased the 1,900 acres that would become the Graves Tract—part of Fulford and most of Sunny Isles—Mr. Graves built a beautiful home in the Lemon City section of Miami, somewhere between the FEC Railway tracks and the bay, between approximately Fifty-ninth and Sixty-fourth Streets. In these views, we are able to appreciate the extent of both the home and the property, complete with two floors, screened-in front porch and open pergola to the left of the porch. *Courtesy collection of Susan Lipp.*

Twenty-Sixth Annual Banquet
of the
H. B. Graves Company, Inc.

Tuesday Evening, January 26th, 1926
Powers Hotel

"Without good company all dainties
Lose their true relish, and, like
painted grapes,
Are only seen, not tasted."

In Rochester, Graves had built a near-dynasty of a furniture business. He was very advanced for his time when it came to the treatment of his employees, instituting one of the first profit-sharing plans in the nation. Early each year the company held its annual banquet, complete with a program with Mr. Graves's picture on the cover. The 1926 banquet was the twenty-sixth annual event. Held at the Powers Hotel, the evening featured a complete dinner with a musical and entertainment program, concluded by the distribution of dividends. *Courtesy collection of Susan Lipp.*

Harvey Baker Graves

During the 1918 boat trip up Biscayne Bay that would result in his huge land purchase, Mr. Graves and his companions were enthralled with the stunning beauty of Biscayne Bay and the rivers that flowed from it. *Courtesy collection of Susan Lipp.*

The reality of the work that was ahead of them began to set in as Mr. Graves (at right) and one of his construction managers assessed the conditions in the mangrove forests that made up much of the area that Graves had purchased. Their work was cut out for them!

From Sandbar *to Sophistication*

South of Sunny Isles, the Biscayne River still flows gently on the west side of today's city, separating the community from the Oleta River State Park and the Biscayne Bay Campus of Florida International University (FIU). This photo, taken on March 22, 1922, is from the collection of Susan Lipp and shows a scene very similar to what one would glimpse today looking west from Sunny Isles Beach, south of 167th Street.

Taken from the veranda of the Sunny Isles office, one could enjoy looking at what was then known as Lone Tree Island. Photograph taken March 22, 1922, possibly by Mr. Graves. *Courtesy collection of Susan Lipp.*

Harvey Baker Graves

Unlike Carl Fisher's Miami Beach, but similar to George Merrick's Coral Gables, Mr. Graves had plans in mind for much of what would become Sunny Isles. Although some of those plans never came to fruition, his wisdom in laying out what would become the city has stood the test of time. On this map, the immensity of the Graves purchase becomes clear, stretching all the way from Arch Creek (at approximately Northeast 135th Street and Biscayne Boulevard in today's North Miami) to Fulford (north of Northeast 163rd Street in today's North Miami Beach). Mr. Graves's ideas were light-years ahead of their time, and many of his concepts are in place today. The relocated Miami Beach Ocean Boulevard is now Collins Avenue and the Sunny Isles Ocean Beach Road is 167th Street on the beach side, 163rd Street on the mainland side. The "proposed bathing pavilion" would eventually be built, albeit not in as grandiose a manner as the image implies. *Courtesy collection of Susan Lipp.*

In this March 22, 1922 view, we are able to see the placement, just off the ocean, of the Sunny Isles sales and management offices. Constructed with screened-in porches, the building remained there until the bathhouse replaced it, circa 1925. *Courtesy collection of Susan Lipp.*

One of the coral rock bridges from the Ocean Beach Boulevard side. The city has declared the remaining bridges historical landmarks, and they will be protected for posterity.

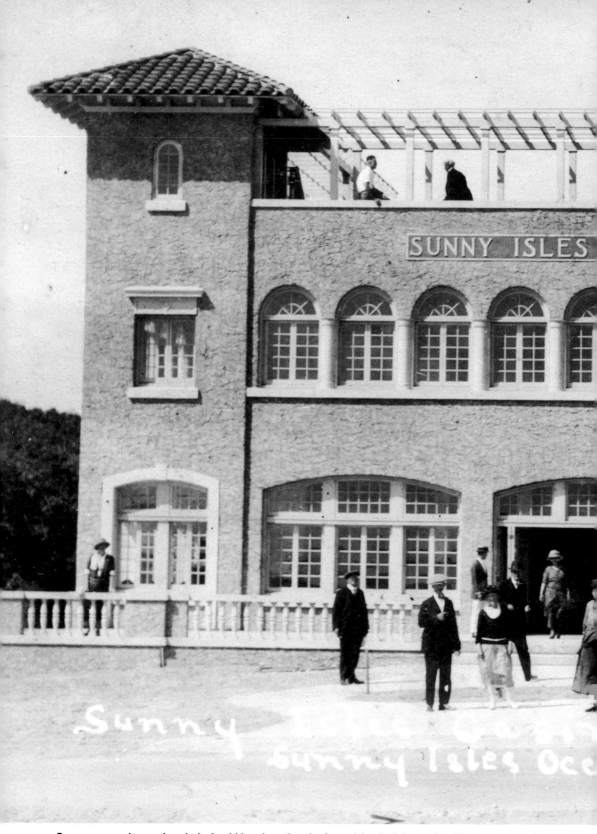

For many years it was thought by local historians that the Sunny Isles Bath House faced Ocean Boulevard (later Collins Avenue). However, that was not the case, as the building actually faced south, and this view allows us to examine the front of the edifice closely. *Courtesy collection of Susan Lipp.*

Beach Co.
Miami, Fla.

From Sandbar *to Sophistication*

A group of excursionists poses before the building. The beach is in front of and behind them, to the right of the building. In this view, we are looking north.

The pier was built in front of the casino in 1936. Although rebuilt several times and much altered since then, the pier remains a fishermen's and sightseer's destination. This picture, used as an advertising piece, was taken just after the pier opened and indicates that Sunny Isles was then still part of North Miami Beach, although the phone number is clearly shown as "Sunny Isles 6"!

Harvey Baker Graves

Although taken a few years past the time frame of this chapter, this picture will give credence to the orientation of the casino and bathhouse (center left). The pier juts out into the Atlantic, the old Ocean Beach Boulevard is still visible and the new Boulevard—now the extension of Collins Avenue through Sunny Isles Beach to the Golden Beach city limits—is on this side of the casino.

It is unknown exactly when this spectacular Sunny Isles publicity picture was taken, but we can clearly see several of the coral rock bridges and the placement of the newly planted and sodded islands. We are looking south, the Ocean Beach Boulevard to our left, the Atlantic Ocean farther east. Excepting several of the bridges, nothing today looks the same in Sunny Isles Beach.

Very late in his long and productive life, Harvey Baker Graves (far right) is posing for what is thought to be the last known photograph of him ever taken in the Miami area, likely shortly before he returned to Rochester for the final time. It is believed that the man at the far left is Harvey Wilbur Graves. The other man on the left is unknown, and the two men behind the fish display tree are the captain and the mate of the fishing boat *Panacea*, based at the Miami Beach Chamber of Commerce docks at Fifth Street and Alton Road. The long-gone Floridian Hotel, built by Miami Beach's founder and builder, Carl Fisher, is visible in the background. *Courtesy collection of Susan Lipp.*

Two

Getting There

Sunny Isles was reached in its earliest years only by boat, and then later by bridge from what would eventually become Bal Harbour Village, north of Miami Beach. Access from the north would come only following completion of the Hollywood Beach Boulevard bridge in the mid-1920s, which allowed motorists to undertake the somewhat less than secure trip down the oceanfront trail from that point.

Mr. Graves knew that he had to have a direct connection to the mainland, so the Sunny Isles Ocean Beach Road (not to be confused with the Ocean Beach Boulevard) was planned to connect Ocean Beach Boulevard on the Sunny Isles side with the Dixie Highway (what would later become Biscayne Boulevard/U.S. 1, not to be confused with the today's Dixie Highway).

The planned Sunny Isles Ocean Beach Road would leave the Dixie Highway at what is today's Northeast 163rd Street in Fulford (NMB today), head east for approximately one half mile, and then curve to the north around the site of Graves's proposed Oleta Point Hotel. Sunny Isles Ocean Beach Road finally curved gently south to the current alignment of today's Sunny Isles Causeway. However, this now looks very little like a causeway because of the development to the north of the roadway.

As noted previously, the events of 1926 followed by the Depression precluded further development, and for some years the area was, while not inaccessible, certainly not easy to reach *Biscayne Country*, Dr. Thelma Peters's fine tome on northeast Dade County, states that "at the time that Graves began his development Sunny Isles was connected by road to both Miami Beach and Fulford." Unfortunately, while Peters provides detailed information on the crossing at Haulover Cut, she gives no additional information on the road from Fulford, and the exact date when Sunny Isles could be reached from the mainland is still uncertain.

Peters also claims that a usable and fully serviceable road was not in place until the late 1930s or the early 1940s, following North Miami Beach's loss of its beachfront property. In any event, a satisfactory roadway must have been in place by 1946. In that year, as noted above, both the Howard Johnson's restaurant and the Golden Strand opened, followed in 1947 by the Trent Motel. It is highly unlikely that ownership would have begun operations on the beach side without a relatively high quality road in place for motorists to use.

Once development began, so did road improvements. Today Sunny Isles Beach is accessed from north and south by Collins Avenue and from the west by an eight-lane Sunny Isles Causeway, a continuation of State Road 826, now one of the county's busiest arterial roadways.

Getting There

613 FISHING AT SUNNY ISLES PIER, MIAMI BEACH, FLORIDA

Above and below: Even before the first motel was built, the fishing pier was in place and the beautiful bridges—built by Harvey Graves—that connected the islands were sightseeing attractions. Dade Countians would use the beach road to get to the pier or would come across the rudimentary causeway to look at the islands and think about the possibility of building a home there. "Idyllic" is probably the least descriptive of the adjectives that could be used to describe the Sunny Isles of an earlier era.

DC-182—Tropical Reflections cast at Sunny Isles, Florida

From Sandbar *to Sophistication*

This incredible aerial view was taken in the very late 1940s or early 1950s. We are above the Graves Tract looking northeast toward Sunny Isles. The roadway running from east to west (left to right) is the Sunny Isles Causeway, and by the total lack of development we can see almost exactly what the area looked like to Harvey Graves when he first explored it.

While getting to the casino might have been an effort, for the gaming-oriented it could be well worth it! Through the courtesy of longtime North Miami resident and member of the Greater North Miami Historical Society Blair Conner, we have proof of the existence of gambling at the casino. This is a photograph of one of the few (possibly the only) casino chips extant from Sunny Isles.

Getting There

Above and below: These two views rank among the rarest and most incredible of the original Graves Tract photographs. Showing the beginnings of a road through the mangroves, both depict the view east from some point on the carved-out roadway of what would someday be the Sunny Isles Causeway. Taken in November 1924, both display wording that indicates that the road is heading across the bay.

From Sandbar *to Sophistication*

Taken in July 1925 from Arch Creek (later Miami Shores—but not today's Miami Shores—and then North Miami) this photograph is a marvelous look at the bridge over the Haulover Cut under construction.

Sometime in the late 1930s, the trailer park—today the south end of Haulover Park—was opened. Built right on the bay and complete with facilities and boat dockage (approximately where the charter fishing boats would later be located), the park is shown in all its newly opened glory.

Getting There

One of the most spectacular "on the way to Sunny Isles" photographs ever taken, this marvelous aerial has us facing west-northwest from just east of Haulover Cut. To the left, on the south side of the cut, is Broussard's seafood restaurant. The old Haulover Bridge is shown in all its glory, right at the ocean edge of the cut, the Sunny Isles Ocean Beach Road clearly shown along the beach. The beloved Lighthouse Restaurant, which burned down in the very early 1960s, is at center right, with the trailer park clearly visible.

The Lighthouse Restaurant, owned and operated for many years by S.D. Macris, was famous for its live turtle and lobster tanks. How the kids loved looking in those tanks! The demise of the restaurant by fire under suspicious circumstances left an empty spot in the hearts of many Miamians who enjoyed the unique atmosphere, the wonderful food and the excellent service.

Captain Ernie Luebbers offered Raytheon fish-finders and a licensed and inspected twin GM diesel yacht. Along with "14 years of safe fishing from these docks," Luebbers made the *Mystery I* one of the most popular boats departing from the Haulover Beach Dock, at 108th Street and Collins Avenue, with fishing all day for six dollars.

Getting There

The fishing boat *Mystery* (a later incarnation of the *Mystery I*) is inbound from its morning excursion in the Atlantic, the Lighthouse Restaurant directly behind the boat and the Haulover Fishing Pier (still extant) in the background jutting out into the ocean.

After the new Haulover Bridge opened in 1950, the former Sunny Isles Ocean Beach Road, already renamed Collins Avenue, was rerouted farther west to its current location. In this view, however, the old road is still extant.

Three

The Motel Era Begins

Mr. Graves foresaw Sunny Isles as both a residential and a resort community, with his building of the casino and the filling in of the several islands as evidence. However, following the cataclysmic events of 1926, the entire region entered a period of quiescence, and activity in the Sunny Isles retreated to near-dormancy.

There were some signs of life, as a few homes were built and the Ocean Beach Boulevard was improved. The Sunny Isles Ocean Beach Road crossing to the mainland would slowly be completed, and the first bridge over the Intracoastal Waterway became a turntable-type operation and was literally hand-operated!

The first hotel to open along what would metamorphose into motel row fifteen years later was the Green Heron at 16801 Collins Avenue, which opened in 1938. Owner John Duff was well known for operating "restricted clientele" hotels on Miami Beach, and the Green Heron was no exception.

Miami Beach—busy and bustling even in the Depression and through World War II, when it was almost completely taken over by the army—had hotels. However, with the end of the war, a number of people began to consider a new type of hostelry, less formal than a hotel, but offering most of the amenities. One of the main differences was that the guests could literally drive their cars right up to the room and not be concerned with giving the cars to a valet parker.

While the open spaces of Sunny Isles were ideal for a wartime artillery range, those same open spaces would also be ideal for trying out the new motel concept. Still, Sunny Isles Beach's first post–World War II inns would open as hotels rather than motels, although they did offer guests free self-parking.

According to Miami historians Jeffrey Levine and Larry Wiggins, the Golden Strand and the Trent would open in the late 1940s, both as hotels. The motels would then follow in rapid succession with the Ocean Palm—the first of the motels to be built on Collins Avenue—opening in 1949. Just prior to the hotel and motel openings, the Howard Johnson Company took the risk, which would pay off handsomely, of opening a full-service restaurant on the southeast corner of 167th Street and Collins in 1946. With the opening of the motels and the success of mainland drive-in restaurants like Colonel Jim's, Kelly's and Jimmy's Hurricane, Bill Breezy opened Scotty's Drive-in at 16301 Collins Avenue, which would later be purchased by the Bookbinder family.

The Motel Era Begins

While the complete story of motel row is covered in chapter five, it is important to note—and memorialize—the initial and original post–Harvey Graves pioneers, for it was they who would start the new boom. They took the initial risks of opening the hotels, motels and restaurants on a stretch of previously deserted and infrequently visited beach with only the casino, the pier and the Green Heron to draw visitors.

Above: The entrance to the Trent Hotel, opened by Gustave Goldberg (aka Tommy Trent), would prove to be highly successful prior to being taken over by—and made part of—the Castaways. This photograph clearly shows the full name of the hotel on the entrance marquee.

Left: Another view of the entrance shows "nothing" north of the hotel, evidence of the fact that the Trent, at 16201 Collins, was one of the first two properties to open in Sunny Isles.

Interior views are generally rare, as most of the hotels and motels preferred to feature the entrance façade and the pool area in their advertising and on their postcards. However, the inviting lobby of the Trent is pictured here.

Compared to today's hotels and motels, the guest rooms of the Trent bordered on stark, but for their day, they were state of the art. The studio bedroom of the hotel was inviting. Note that, just after the hotel's opening, there was no television in the room!

The Motel Era Begins

The Green Heron was the first hostelry to be built on what would become Sunny Isles Beach but what was still North Miami Beach at the time it opened. The brochure pointedly notes that "patronage is carefully restricted" and that the hotel caters to a "limited number of discriminating guests," those being catchphrases for the fact that no members of the Jewish faith were welcome. The hotel would operate into the early 1960s, although it is likely that a later and more enlightened ownership did not continue the anti-Semitic policy of the hotel's original owner.

The golden strand Hotel and

the

Although this is a later view, the Golden Strand, at 179th and Collins, was one of the two original hotels of the motel row era. By the time this photograph was taken, the hotel had more than doubled in size.

s, Miami Beach, Fla.

el that is PERSONALLY YOURS

In later years the bathing suits would become bikinis and brevity would be the norm, but the Sunny Isles cheesecake photos (using beautiful women as props to promote the glories of winter in south Florida) of the late 1940s featured girls showing—of all things—their thighs!

Although some of the motels south of 167th Street were in place, this early 1950s aerial view includes the casino (at right, just west of the pier). With the exception of the shops on 167th Street and the homes on Atlantic Isle, a vast amount of acreage was still completely untouched. What would become Eastern Shores, just north of the causeway, was not even a glimmer in the eyes of the developers at the time.

One of the most interesting views of early Sunny Isles, taken just after the Suez's 1953 opening, this photograph looks north from the Suez Motel at 18225 Collins and shows both the Sherwood and the Blue Grass Motels. The reader will note that Collins Avenue is clearly two lanes!

From Sandbar *to Sophistication*

Above and below: Norman Giller, principal of the architectural firm of Norman M. Giller and Associates, was responsible for the design of many of the Sunny Isles motels. Ira Giller, his son and partner, has provided original drawings of several of the motels. The Neptune Motel drawing shows the King of the Sea as part of the front façade of the building. The drawing of the Thunderbird was remarkably accurate when the prototype was built, and the building looked almost exactly as shown in this rendering.

The Motel Era Begins

The Ocean Palm (15795 Collins), designed by Norman Giller, would open in 1949. To the left of the building, the sign for the inn bears the words "Motor Hotel," the "motel" appellation not yet in use.

From Sandbar *to Sophistication*

The Gould was built in 1950 and was quite small. It would later be taken over by the Desert Inn and incorporated into their operation. As with the Ocean Palm photographs, the Gould's publicity scenes allow us to see both the building and its east side. *Courtesy collection of Larry Wiggins.*

The Motel Era Begins

MIAMI BEACH

EL **Sombrero** MOTEL

EL SOMBRERO

DIRECTLY ON THE OCEAN

AT

174th ST. and COLLINS AVE. (A1A)

MIAMI BEACH

El Sombrero was at 17451 Collins Avenue. Both postcards and brochures are exceedingly rare, so turning up this advertising piece was like finding buried treasure. The motel was apparently subsumed into another property quite early in Sunny Isles Beach's history.

While the motel era was in its infancy, residences on the Baker-created islands were respites from the hubbub and tumult of one of America's greatest resort areas just coming to life. The home shown here is a perfect example of south Florida as a tropical paradise.

Four

More Than Just the Motels

In its earliest years, Sunny Isles offered only the casino, with little—if anything—else to provide either amusement or a reason to venture "up" (from Miami Beach) or "over" (from the mainland) there. As noted previously, the pier opened in 1936, the Green Heron in 1938, and a hardy few built homes either on the west side of Collins Avenue or on the islands created by Mr. Graves.

With World War II came the artillery range, but at the end of the war a new era arrived. Food and beverage operators, theater owners, dress and clothing store managers and entrepreneurs of numerous other stripes and persuasions would see the advantages in being among the first to start a business in Sunny Isles.

Sunny Isles would become a "must" for Miami's residents, who showed their visitors motel row or "the strip" (as it was often called). Those excursions were frequently made at or during dining times and restaurateurs found Sunny Isles enticing, even though, for many coming to see the motels, it was "a schlep" (a long trip) from much of Dade or Broward Counties.

Besides the restaurants, numerous stores would open including two large auction galleries, and Eddie Albert (not the actor) would become famous locally with his "Eddie Albert's Men's Store" commercials that he and his son would sing. Innumerable gift and sundry shops would dot the landscape, with gas stations, real estate offices and eventually strip shopping centers becoming a part of the area.

As the number of cars and tourists increased exponentially, so did the businesses that would accommodate them. Over time Sunny Isles would have banks, a bowling alley, a car wash, a miniature golf course and driving range and low- and high-rise apartments and condominiums. It had become a fun place and a true amusement destination, both for the tourists and the locals. They mingled in the stores and restaurants and enjoyed the sun, sand, surf and sights as they ate, shopped or vacationed in a very special place at a very special moment in time.

More Than Just the Motels

Before heading for Scotty's, it was a good idea to get the car washed, and Cars-a-Wash-in, at 301 Sunny Isles Ocean Beach Boulevard, was the ideal place to do so, especially for those who wanted to impress the beautiful young car hops (as well as their dates!). Both the Scotty's and the Cars-a-Wash-in photographs were taken on December 21, 1955. *Scotty's photograph courtesy collection of Larry Wiggins.*

In 1962 Sunny Isles Bowling Center opened at 18330 Collins. It was a modern and luxurious venue in its heyday—complete with a snack bar—an exciting place for children and adults alike to enjoy an afternoon or evening. *Courtesy Larry Wiggins collection.*

VISIT
GOLFLAND
DRIVING RANGE
at

17100 Collins Avenue
Miami Beach
WI 5-2571

- Sand Traps
- Covered Tees
- Professional Instruction

GOLFLAND

36 HOLES OF
MINIATURE GOLF

VISIT OUR OTHER LOCATIONS

6900 Collins Avenue
16300 Collins Avenue
17100 Collins Avenue
Board walk, Hollywood Beach

*"Florida's finest
miniature golf Chain"*

Miniature golf was always fun, and Golfland's owners billed their properties as "Florida's finest miniature golf chain." Two of their mini courses were in Sunny Isles, one at 16300 Collins, the other at 17100 Collins, both on the west side of the street. The driving range, complete with a golf pro available for lessons, was also at 17100.

More Than Just the Motels

The name alone brings back warm memories, and when we think about fried clams, chocolate chip ice cream, frankfurters and so many other things, Howard Johnson's comes immediately to mind. Though the names of the people in these two photographs have been lost in time, for many years this HoJo's was a fixture on the southeast corner of Northeast 167th Street and Collins. While we don't know what the celebrated event was that day, we can certainly see that the Thursday Chicken Fry was $1.49 and seconds of chicken were available for those who desired them.

In Sunny Isles history, it is rare to see people rather than buildings as the object of the camera lens. This fine view presents the HoJo's food prep staff, all smiling happily in their new and immaculate kitchen.

Arthur Courshon, longtime Miami Beach booster and chairman of Jefferson National Bank (JNB) on Miami Beach's 41st Street, believed as strongly in Sunny Isles's future as he did in Miami Beach's. In the very early 1970s, Courshon opened a JNB in Sunny Isles, with his good friend Norman M. Giller serving as vice-chairman and president. This is one of few letterheads that still exist. *Bank photograph courtesy Ira Giller, Giller and Giller, Inc.*

NORMAN M. GILLER
Vice Chairman and President

JEFFERSON ⬥ NATIONAL BANK
★ ★ ★ ★
AT SUNNY ISLES
290 SUNNY ISLES BOULEVARD
MIAMI BEACH, FLORIDA 33160 • TELEPHONE (305) 949-2121

A SUBSIDIARY OF JEFFERSON BANCORP, INC.

More Than Just the Motels

As was the norm for so many years, Gusar, like almost all other drugstores in the country, had a "fountain," a pseudonym for a lunch counter. However, Gusar's curved counter was unique!

Among the several gas stations in Sunny Isles was Standard Oil at 17800 Collins. Shown here on November 11, 1958, it is evident that the station was close to brand new.

It was December 16, 1952, and quite evidently the Texaco station, at 19190 Collins on the west side of the street was not overwhelmed. At this time, although plans to build were underway, a good bit of Sunny Isles was still not developed.

More Than Just the Motels

In May 1958 Loew's would open its 170th Street Theatre, and the marquee announced that it would be "Florida's Finest Theatre." For a few years it was, and people from all over north Dade County would trek to Sunny Isles to enjoy the first-run offerings. While the building is still there, it is no longer a theater and is now used for other purposes.

From Sandbar *to* *Sophistication*

Another view from just south of the Loew's marquee. Taken on April 25, 1958, in this image we can clearly see the Driftwood and the Gould Motels on the east side of Collins Avenue.

The Sinclair station was just north of 167th Street on the west side of Collins. Although this photo is undated, the automobiles in the view give us a circa 1958 time frame.

More Than Just the Motels

On May 28, 1955, an unknown photographer snapped this scene of 167th Street, looking west from just east of Collins Avenue. Crawford's Drugs is visible at the immediate right, and farther west are numerous stores serving the local populace. The famous Lime House Restaurant's sign extends up from the building just about in the center of the photo.

The Champagne Steak House was at 468 Sunny Isles Boulevard just east of the long-lasting Lagoon Restaurant. Shown on November 12, 1956, the restaurant's tenure in Sunny Isles was rather short.

Arthur Wilde's, at 193rd and Collins, was for many years a great favorite, and it would survive until the building of the Marco Polo necessitated its removal.

For Your Dining Pleasure . . . Don't Forget To Visit The . . .

BLACK ANGUS
RESTAURANT AND LOUNGE
AIR CONDITIONED

17700 COLLINS AVENUE - MIAMI BEACH, FLORIDA
2650 NO. FEDERAL HIGHWAY, FORT LAUDERDALE, FLORIDA

Char-Broiled
SIRLOIN STEAK DINNER
$1.69

THIS IS
NO BUM STEER

"We can sell our steaks at this low price because we have an uncle who is a Cattle Rustler."

Black Angus was at 17700 Collins and the other side of this interesting advertising piece—offering a steak dinner for $1.69!—tells us that the Black Angus was "A Friendly Rendezvous for Nice People." One has to wonder who made the decision as to who was—or wasn't—"nice"!

More Than Just the Motels

Grandma's Kitchen and Grandpa's Bar had several Greater Miami locations. The Sunny Isles store was opened in the original casino as this clearly shows and there are photographs showing the restaurant at that location as early as 1958. The Stewarts, who owned Grandma's Kitchen, also opened the Pier Deck right next door at the very east end of 167th Street.

Dagwood's opened in the late 1960s at 17024 Collins, probably a little too close to the Rascal House! Presenting the same type of Jewish-style (not Kosher) deli-oriented menu as the Rascal, Dagwood's, advertising "a luxurious feeling in an informal atmosphere," struggled for a few years, finally closing in the early 1980s.

SUN CITY RESTAURANT, INC.

ORIGINAL SAM & DOROTHY

Picciolo

ITALIAN-AMERICAN RESTAURANT

TERRACE DINING   **AT SUN**

Sam and Dorothy Picciolo (pronounced "peach-uh-low") were famous for their longtime Miami Beach operation at 136 Collins Avenue, but almost lost in the mists of time is the memory of their short-lived operation in Sun City Motel at 17350 Collins on the west side of the street. It is likely that they opened the Sunny Isles store

DINING ROOM   COMPLETELY AIR CONDITIONED

MOTEL, 17350 COLLINS AVE., SUNNY ISLES, FLA.

when Angie and Fred Buoncervello, also famous for their Miami Beach restaurants (Angie and Fred's), leased the 136 Collins Avenue store.

From Sandbar *to Sophistication*

Most Miami-area historians know only that Wolfie Cohen opened the Rascal House, at 172nd and Collins, to rave reviews. For many years, the place was mobbed, becoming one of the fifty highest-grossing non-chain restaurants in the country. But what people don't know is that the restaurant opened as Pumpernik's, another famous Miami and Miami Beach deli-style eatery. Wolfie, moving quickly, bought Pumpernik's within a year of its opening. The lovely ladies holding the Pumpernik's menus in the upper photo are probably doing so in the last week prior to Wolfie's takeover and name change to "Rascal House." Wolfie, in the meantime, sits serenely at the counter, likely somewhat aware that the restaurant he would take over would help catapult him to the riches and fame that he earned from his many years in the business.

More Than Just the Motels

This aerial view, taken on May 28, 1955, shows the Rascal House building (left center). On the right is the strip shopping center where Jahn's Ice Cream Parlor would become famous for offering "the kitchen sink."

Shown on the corner of 172nd Street and Collins, on May 28, 1955, the Pumpernik's name was gone and the Rascal House sign was in place. Wolfie, known as "the Rascal," earned that moniker for such antics as giving away food for free on opening day. Harry Thal, formerly of Miami Beach's Epicure Market, remembers the event and the crowds, which grew through the day as word spread. Those crowds never let up!

It is July 10, 1957, and the photographer is in a plane (or maybe the Goodyear blimp!). The view is south from approximately 186th and Collins, with private homes clearly visible directly below the aircraft. There are only two strip shopping centers visible on the west side of Collins.

More Than Just the Motels

Another aerial view, this one circa 1955, looks north from south of 167th Street, the pier clearly visible but much of the beachfront and the west side of Collins still unbuilt upon, although the shops on the north side of 167th Street are already in place.

The Greater Miami Beach Motel Association no longer exists, but, at one time, they represented almost every motel on "the strip." On November 13, 1957, their brand new billboard on the southeast corner of U.S. 1 (Biscayne Boulevard) and Northeast 163rd Street was photographed. Even then, according to the display, there were "over 5000 rooms" in the largest concentration of motels in the country, stretching from 156th Street and Collins on the south (where Haulover Park ends) to 195th and Collins on the north (where the city of Golden Beach begins).

An absolutely stunning view of Sunny Isles, this low-level aerial was taken on September 27, 1962, from just above the Lagoon Restaurant at the east end of the Intracoastal Waterway bridge coming over from the mainland. To the right of the Lagoon is the Champagne Steakhouse, next to which are long-gone tennis courts. The 170th Street shopping center can be seen upper center, behind which the marquee of the Dunes is clearly visible on the other side of Collins Avenue. Very little of what is shown in this photograph is extant today.

Five

Motel Row

U nquestionably, the heart of Sunny Isles history was the motel era, which effectively began in 1950, although the Golden Strand, Green Heron, Ocean Palm and Trent opened prior to that year. In 1950 at least twelve motels opened, including the Atlantique, Blue Seas, one of the Castaways units, the Gould, the Gregory, the Heathwood, Kimberly, Olympia, Sandy Shores, Sea Breeze, Sun City, Sunny Isles, Waikiki and Windward. And with that, the floodgates for new motel openings were open wide.

Although a few of the opening dates are unknown because the records have sadly been lost or discarded through the years, what is known is that the strip from 156th Street to 195th Street on both sides of Collins would become laden with some of the most interesting, unique and fascinating architecture in U.S. history. Some of the accoutrements of the motels—including horses and carriages, circular stairways to nowhere, Bedouin figures standing eternally outside a motel, Chinese-oriented architecture and soaring triangular shaped roofs—have become part and parcel of both architectural and Florida history. Their names range from Chateau to Fountainhead, from Suez and Monaco to Olympia. All credit is due to the builders who had the faith in the future to construct these unique inns and welcoming beacons of hospitality.

Many people lament the passing of motel row, but the fact is that without casinos very few—if any—people were willing to invest the funds necessary either to upgrade the existing motels or to build new ones. The value of the land, some of which still belonged to the original owners at the time the property was sold, had soared exponentially.

For many years, Sunny Isles's motel row was a magical place, and whether one was a tourist or a local there were always exciting events and people to be seen, wonderful places at which to eat and new friends to be made. More than a few marital unions occurred because couples met on motel row.

It was a moment that—at least in south Florida— will never be recaptured. All of us, whether casual readers or historians, must remember with gratitude that that moment occurred, and having lived through it, it has enriched our memories and our lives.

Although rarely remarked upon, the Belmont Park Motel at 174th Street and Collins Avenue was built in another of the unique designs that has helped to draw so much interest to Sunny Isles Beach's fascinating architectural history. With a head house in the Mount Vernon colonial style, complete with a four-columned porch, the motel units were arrayed behind the hotel. This very rare flyer, published shortly after opening, offers rooms at the 220-unit motel for four dollars per day, two in a room, six dollars daily with kitchenette!

For many years the Sunny Isles motel owners considered themselves to be in Miami Beach, even though Miami Beach ended at 87th Terrace and unincorporated Sunny Isles began at 156th Street, with Surfside, Bal Harbour and Haulover Park in between. The Argosy, at 17425 Collins, and the Aztec, at 159th and Collins, featured the Miami Beach location, although the Aztec mentioned Sunny Isles in this mid-1970s brochure.

Motel Row

The Bali was at 16935 Collins Avenue. One of the smaller properties on motel row, it was designed by Norman Giller and opened in 1953.

The Beachcomber, at 189th Street, advertised the Bikini Room Night Club and a "galaxy of features." Unusual to see, this pre-opening advertising postcard shows the motel as originally envisioned.

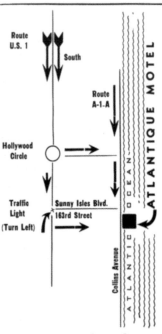

The Atlantique would eventually become part of the Castaways complex. When this flyer was published, circa 1957, one could enjoy the sun and fun of Sunny Isles and Miami Beach for $2.50 per day per person, two in a room, with, among other amenities, free ice cubes at all hours!

Motel Row

Bimini Bay, at 17480 Collins, was one of the smaller west-side-of-Collins motels. Mostly unremarked upon because their usually much larger siblings were on the ocean (east) side of Collins, the "west side" motels should also be noted and remembered.

The Blue Grass, at 183rd and Collins, was one of the very few oceanside motels that had separate buildings with motel rooms behind the head house, as seen on the left.

From Sandbar *to Sophistication*

Several motels had "Blue" in their names. Pictured here are the Blue Mist, at 19111 Collins, with its fanciful aqua-maidens holding up the front porte-cochere and manager Moishe Poopick standing in front, and the Blue Seas, shown from the ocean side in March 1967.

Motel Row

The staircase to nowhere at the Bon-Aire on the Sea at 18145 Collins always attracted interest. It was a fanciful and unique design, uncopied by any of the other motels. This photograph, taken in 1954, exemplifies the architectural singularity of Sunny Isles.

The Buccaneer, at 19275 Collins Avenue, featured this beautiful sailing ship mural on the front of the building. This photograph, taken by a guest in 1953, is a true "find" for any student of Sunny Isles and its history.

On July 14, 1953, several of the motels that would become the Castaways were pictured here in an aerial view, with a new building under construction. Across the street the entrance to one of the islands can be seen.

Joe Hart's final triumph as owner of the Castaways was the building of the huge (for its day) addition on the east side of Collins Avenue. The edifice became the home of the Wreck Bar, with its beautiful go-go dancers aptly named the Wreckettes. Taken several years after the previous photograph, this view gives a larger perspective and shows the new building under construction with Atlantic Isle to the left and 167th Street to the right.

From Sandbar *to Sophistication*

Not since Roberto had mixed drinks, told jokes and worn fanciful outfits and fruit-laden headpieces at the Edward Hotel on South Beach in the 1930s and '40s had there been a bartender to match him—until the day that Stanley the Great reported to work for the first time at the Castaways' Tahiti Bar, remaining as a fixture for almost twenty years, when the hotel closed. On New Year's Eve 2004, Stanley would make his last public appearance as bartender at the home of Cindy Seipp and Al Diaz, as flamboyant and "Great" as ever. Sadly to report, Stanley the Great died in early 2005.

Motel Row

The Wreck Bar was one of Sunny Isles's hottest hot spots, and it was always a safe and happy place, usually due to the attentiveness of its assistant manager, the late Johnny Pachivas. An eighth-degree karate black belt, Pachivas—unless the occasion required otherwise—was both a gentleman and a gentle man. Needless to say, Johnny's reputation preceded him and it was rare that anyone was foolish enough to become nasty or obstreperous at the Wreck Bar.

The Colonial Inn was at 181st Street, and this circa 1959 image shows the entire property including both buildings and the parking entrances.

Another of the rarely remarked upon properties was the Cavalier at 175th and Collins. Built in 1950, the motel had several individual buildings with "all rooms facing east to ocean."

From Sandbar *to Sophistication*

The Chateau covered five acres on the ocean at 191st Street. It was opened in 1960 and was always considered one of the finer properties on the strip, though it was eventually overshadowed when the Marco Polo opened next door. The lobby, shown below, was a good bit larger than most of the other Sunny Isles motels' reception areas.

Motel Row

The Coral Seas was at 16201 Collins. Designed by Norman Giller it opened in 1950. The unique two-and-a-half-story towers on either side of the front entrance were another Giller innovation.

Desert Inn was ten blocks north of the Coral Seas, at 172nd Street. One of the larger low-rise properties, it featured a mule-drawn wagon on the north side of the entrance. This pair of views shows both the front and the back of the 1954-built motel.

From Sandbar *to Sophistication*

The Driftwood was another unusual building, the second floor card/recreation/entertainment room built with a curve and the large namesake piece of flotsam attached to the front facing of the motel above the lobby doors. A Giller creation, the motel opened in 1954 at 17121 Collins.

Unquestionably one of the favored motels on the strip, the Dunes was, until the Newport and the Marco Polo opened, a hot spot. Owned for many years by Al Pollack, the Dunes was at 17001 Collins and was designed by architect Melvin Grossman in what is now known as MiMo, the Miami Modern style of architecture. The property opened in 1955.

Motel Row

At almost opposite ends of the strip, the Golden Arrow was at 15600 Collins and was the very first motel on the bay (west) side if one was coming from Miami Beach and had driven past Haulover Park. These views depict not only the exterior of the inn but also the 1950s guest room.

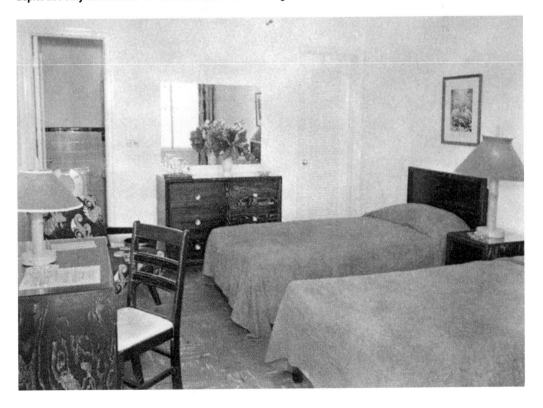

Golden Beach Apartments stand at 19475 Collins and just a few properties south of the Golden Beach city limits.

The Golden Gate was at the north end of the strip and was the next to last property at 193rd Street, with only the Last Frontier Motel farther north. The Golden Gate was a sizable and formidable property. Built on both sides of Collins Avenue, it bore the title of hotel rather than motel and covered twenty acres. Although under the management of John F. Duff Jr., the days of "restricted clientele" had passed and unlike the brochure for the Green Heron, also managed by Duff, no mention is made that the guests had to be suitably "selected." Incredibly, a tunnel under Collins Avenue connected the properties.

Another view of the Golden Gate Hotel.

From Sandbar *to Sophistication*

This spectacular January 10, 1967 photograph shows the Golden Gate (curved building, pool prominent on the right) on both sides of the street, the Last Frontier just north of it and beyond that Sunny Isles's neighbor, the entirely residential community of Golden Beach. At the very top of the photo, the first of the Hallandale Beach (Broward County) high-rises can be seen.

Motel Row

BOTTLE PRICES FOR ROOM SERVICE

BLENDS

CARSTAIRS – QTS.	$6.50
SEAGRAM'S – 7 CROWN – 5TH	6.00
LORD CALVERT – 5TH	6.50
FOUR ROSES – 5TH	6.00

BOURBON S (STRAIGHT) – 5THS

WALKER'S DE LUXE	6.50
OLD CROW	6.50
EARLY TIMES	6.50

BOURBONS (BONDED) – 5THS

OLD GRANDAD	8.00
OLD FORESTER	8.00
OLD FITZGERALD	8.00
KENTUCKY TAVERN	8.00
I.W. HARPER	8.00

CANADIAN WHISKEY – 5THS

CANADIAN CLUB	7.50
SEAGRAM'S V.O.	7.50

SODA'S   SPLITS .25   QUARTS .75

SCOTCH

HAIG & HAIG – 5 STAR	8.00
BLACK & WHITE	8.00
MARTIN'S VVO	8.00
BALLANTINES	8.00
TEACHERS	8.00
DEWARS WHITE LABEL	8.00
CUTTY SARK	8.00
J & B	8.00
JOHNNIE WALKER RED	8.00
JOHNNIE WALKER BLACK	9.50
BELL 12 Y.O.	10.00
GRANT'S 12 Y.O.	10.00
CHIVAS REGAL	10.00
HAIG & HAIG PINCH	10.00

GIN

GORDON – QTS.	6.50
SEAGRAMS – 5TH	5.50
WALKERS – 5TH	5.50
BEEFEATER – 5TH	7.00
HOUSE OF LORD'S – BOOTHS – 5TH.	7.00

VODKA

SMIRNOFF – QTS. – 80°	6.50
TAAKA – 5TH – 80°	5.00

RUM – (5THS)

BACARDI – PUERTO RICAN	6.75
BACARDI – CUBAN	6.75
MYERS	6.75

LIQUOR MAY BE PURCHASED ANY DAY FROM 11:00 A.M. TO 1:00 A.M.
EXCEPT SUNDAY – 5:00 P.M. TO 1:00 A.M.

PLEASE CALL ROOM SERVICE BEVERAGE

Being a hotel, the Golden Gate had full dining room and room service. This is the circa 1960–62 room service liquor by the bottle price list, but everything is relative, as hotel rooms at that time were about twelve dollars per night per person!

The Golden Nugget, with its angled and sloping roof, was an architectural gem in terms of construction. The motel was built in 1956 at 18641 Collins.

Another of the west side of Collins smaller properties, the Gregory was named for its owner-manager Gregory Codomo. The Gregory was another of the 1950s group of motels that helped to open the doors for all that was to come.

Shown at night, the inventively named Hawaiian Isle is complete with what looks like a 1960s Dodge in front of it, along with the tiki torches and the Polynesian mask motif. The motel, at 17601 Collins, was a longtime favorite that attracted people simply because of its unusual appearance.

Motel Row

The Heathwood was another of the low-key motels that featured barbeques and shuffleboard rather than glitzier activities. It boasted a strikingly beautiful lounge, named the Stowaway. The motel, at 18671 Collins, claimed it was "famed for friendliness." The upper photo was taken January 14, 1953.

Holiday Inn would eventually join the crowd on Sunny Isles Beach, and at one point there were at least three motels bearing the HI banner, this one at 180th Street. None of them were built new; rather they took over existing properties, or the property owners became Holiday Inn franchisees.

Holiday Inn®

180th Street
MIAMI BEACH, FLA.

REG. U. S. PAT. OFF

From Sandbar *to Sophistication*

The Magic Isle was at 16875 Collins and in the lower image the Sunny Isles pier is clearly visible in the background.

Motel Row

At 158th Street, the Kimberly was two blocks north of the north end of Haulover Park, and this image is one of the very few visuals in which one actually sees the refurbishing of a motel. One view shows the original August Swarz–designed 1950 hotel with the convertible in front; the other, taken in what appears to be the early to mid-1960s shows the new façade. The hotel would go through several owners and name changes, becoming, through the years, the Riviera Beach Resort, American Beach Resort and a Days Inn.

Kimberly Hotel, Pool and Cabana Club, Miami Beach

From Sandbar *to Sophistication*

The Lido Beach Motel

AAA

MBM GREATER MIAMI BEACH MOTEL ASSOCIATION

Miami Beach

Directly on the Ocean at 173rd Street Route A1A
Phone North Dade 6-2691

100% Air-Conditioned

ALL MOTEL ROOMS

2 50

PER PERSON DOUBLE

MAY 1st TO DEC. 1st
NO EXTRA CHARGES

Informality

You'll Live it Up
AT THE LIDO
(and love every
moment.)

HOW TO GET TO THE LIDO BEACH MOTEL

DANIA
Route U. S. 1
Route A1A
Hollywood Circle
Hallandale
LIDO BEACH MOTEL
163rd St.
Collins Ave.
79th St. Causeway
Lincoln Road

DOWN U. S. 1, TURN LEFT AT DANIA, HOLLYWOOD, HALLANDALE, OR 163RD ST. TO A1A AND TO THE LIDO RIGHT ON THE OCEAN AT 173RD ST.

Top Ocean Front Luxury
FREE

- PRIVATE CRYSTAL POOL
- HUGE PRIVATE BEACH
- TROPICAL SUNDECKS
- SHUFFLE BOARDS
- WIENER ROASTS
- FREE MOVIES AND ENTERTAINMENT
- SURF FISHING FROM YOUR DOORSTEP
- PARKING AT YOUR DOOR

Coffee Shop
Motel Rooms and Efficiency Apartments
Phone. Radio and T.V. in Rooms

MIAMI BEACH'S MOST FAMOUS RESTAURANT-SHOPPING CENTER
Golf Course and Driving Range, Just Seconds Away.

You could "live it up" at the Lido, or at least that's what the flyer tells us. Another of the wonderful five dollars per day, per couple offers, the Lido Beach Motel was at 173rd Street, just a block west of Rascal House.

Motel Row

The Mandalay, at 162nd and Collins, was designed by Melvin Grossman and opened in 1952. Among the amenities, guests received orange juice, wiener roasts at poolside (hot dogs were so good that way!), cocktails, shuffleboard, movies, water shows, poolside photos and a deck chair—all free!

An incredibly rare image, this shows not only the front of the Malibu at 16100 Collins but also the waterway behind the motel. Looking carefully at that photograph one can see one of the Graves-built bridges with the Castaways behind it. The Malibu opened in 1951.

Another of the smaller oceanside properties, the Malvern, at 17475 Collins, was originally managed by S.J. Kaufman, and within a few years it would become the Ed-Mar Court.

tiful OCEANFRONT Motel

From Sandbar *to Sophistication*

The Marco Polo was built by longtime Miami Beach hotelier and real estate magnate (as well as Miami Beach High graduate) Bennett Lifter in 1967. Still open and still doing well, the Marco was among the last built of the Sunny Isles hostelries. With thirteen floors, Lifter's Marco Polo Resort Hotel, along with Irving Pollack's Newport, brought new blood and new life to the strip. The hotel and one of the beautifully decorated oceanview guest rooms are pictured here.

MARINER
MOTEL
17320 COLLINS AVENUE
Miami Beach, Florida
ON ROUTE AIA

AND
Seneca Shores Apts...

The Mariner and the Seneca Shores Apartments were under the direction of Joseph Rosenfeld and they advertised together, as shown here. The motel was at 17320 Collins, the apartments just across the street on the ocean.

Another of the unique and interesting façades was that of the Neptune. (See chapter three for Norman Giller's architectural rendering of the motel.) As can be seen here, the King of the Sea sits on his watery throne on the left side while a diving mermaid is on the right. The motel, at 15995 Collins, opened in 1952.

From Sandbar *to Sophistication*

For more than ten years, the Newport was the number one happenin' place on the strip. It was the home of both the Seven Seas Lounge—which featured great old-time rock-and-roll acts such as Ike and Tina Turner, Little Richard, The Mob and Chuck Berry—and the Pub Restaurant, which, with its separate ground lease, was presided over by Wolfie Cohen, Saul Kaplan, Al Nemets and Mario Talucci. The Newport was, without exaggeration, the busiest property on the strip. The upper view looks west toward the mainland, the Newport (formerly Sunny Isles) pier at left. The lower view, taken from a guest room, looks east toward the Atlantic, the pier visible on the right from the window. Both photos were taken in April 1967.

Motel Row

The Newport (16700 Collins Avenue) from the front looking northeast. The lighthouse, which actually operated, was purely decorative. The single-story extension of the tower housed the Pub Restaurant and the Seven Seas Lounge.

When he worked as maitre d' at the Embers on Miami Beach, Mario Talucci was so well known that he would receive letters addressed simply "Mario, Miami Beach, Florida." With the opening of the Pub, Talucci was given the same position as he held at the Embers and with his warm smile, deep voice and personal greetings, he remained one of the area's most beloved restaurauteurs. Shown here to the left of Don Rickles, Mario makes the great comedian and his mother feel comfortable at the Pub.

The walkway on the east side of the Ocean Palm Motor Hotel.

Motel Row

The Ocean Shore was at 18601 Collins. The motel advertised "a striking semi-tropic setting" and advised prospective guests that they were "Completely pollen free for relief of Hay Fever and Rose Fever."

The Olympia was built in 1950 and remodeled in 1989. Located at 15701 Collins, it was the third motel from the north end of Haulover Park and is shown here on April 7, 1966.

From Sandbar *to Sophistication*

Prince Royal Motel was at 15820 Collins on the west side of the street. Owned by Leonore and Sam Racusin, the bridge to one of the original Harvey Graves islands is visible at the right edge of this photograph.

This October 27, 1960 view is a close-up of the front of the Pan American Motel, originally opened in 1952 at 17875 Collins Avenue. This motel was the last of the few Sunny Isles properties to attempt to maintain a restricted clientele guest base, with Jewish people not welcome.

Motel Row

Many people are in disbelief when told that, at one time in the past, declining to have people as guests because of their religion or color was accepted, although illegal. This is the reverse of a Pan American Motel postcard and along with the wording in the brochures the postcard makes clear, in the last line of the copy on the left, that the motel provided "Informal living for a selected clientele."

An almost lost sport or pastime, shuffleboard was one of the most popular games of the hotel-motel-resort era of the 1930s, '40s and '50s, both in the New York State Catskills and in Florida, where it was followed with almost religious fervor in places such as St. Petersburg and at Salvadore Park in Coral Gables. Here a guest at the Pan American prepares to push the disc hoping to win another game.

From Sandbar *to Sophistication*

As shown here, the Pan American was a beautiful and well-maintained property, the only downside being the foolishness of its clearly prejudiced policy regarding who was and wasn't welcome there.

The Reviva at Golden Shores was owned by Stanley Orvis and was at 19090 Collins. On the west side of the street it was a lovely and quiet property and attracted a fair share of seasonal rather than short-term guests.

Motel Row

Just south of the Reviva, at 19050 Collins, was Robert Hutchison's Rovern. This property, with its small, casual one-story U-shaped layout also saw a majority of seasonal guests each year, people returning from the north and staying at these and other smaller, quieter facilities for several months at a time.

The Safari was another of the properties with unusual motifs. At 17749 Collins, it offered guests the opportunity to have pictures taken atop the white elephant in front of the building, following which they could enjoy a swim in the motel's pool. Here a guest relaxes on a chaise lounge, while another sits on the low diving board and a third prepares to dive from the high board.

The Carlos Schoeppl–designed Sahara opened in 1953 with an Egyptian/Bedouin theme, the famous camels in front of the motel drawing onlookers and photographers for many years. At 18335 Collins, the Sahara was one of the had-to-be-seen locales.

This Sahara brochure features a cartoon of an Arabian rug, its swami passenger and his bag at their destination, clearly noted by the sign, which says, "Miami Beach or bust."

A brochure from the Santa Anita, at 16421 Collins, features an early 1950s Cadillac and a February 1953 date stamp inside the folder.

Sandy Shores Motel was directly on the ocean at 16251 Collins and this property, designed by Charles Melov, opened in 1950. A set of three views gives the reader an indication of the proximity to the ocean, the appearance of the front of the building and the swimming pool.

The Sea Court, at 16200 Collins Avenue, was another of the west side of Collins operations. This marvelous pair of views shows us not only the front of the building but also an excellent vista of the waterway behind the motel. The boat *Chick*, named for beloved Miami Beach High graduate David "Chicky" Rogers, is pulling into one of the docking spaces.

From Sandbar *to Sophistication*

For many years, Marcella's Restaurant on West Dixie Highway in North Miami was a great favorite of the locals. Eventually, Marcella would branch into catering and personal appearances at various hotels, motels and other venues, and her appearances were always anticipated by those fortunate enough to enjoy her great Italian food. On April 26, 1959, the Sea Breeze, at 16151 Collins, brought Marcella in to prepare a complimentary pizza lunch for the guests. Her truck, with Marcella waving to the camera, is shown in front of the motel. After setting up her tables and ovens, Marcella personally served slices of pizza to the guests.

Motel Row

Built in 1952, the Sherwood Court was of the semi- or modified colonial style motels, with a columned head house and motel rooms in the rear. The motel, at 18275 Collins, with nothing yet built to the south, is depicted here on April 23, 1953.

The Suez, at 18215, was almost next door to the Sherwood Court. Another of the Middle Eastern–themed properties, the Suez fit in with the Dunes, Sahara, Safari and others. Norman M. Giller was the architect of this unusual 1954 motel.

Motel Row

The Sunny Isle Motel would also be known as the Sunny Isles Motel, and for whatever reason the "s" at the end of the word "Isles" did not always appear on brochures or postcards. Constructed in 1950, the motel was at 16525 Collins and was one of the first facilities to become part of the Castaways. A view of the buildings is shown here, the Howard Johnson's in front of the motel building at right. In the far right corner of the photo, the original Graves-built casino appears in one of its restaurant incarnations.

Unlike the great 1926 hurricane and Hurricane Andrew in 1992, photos of 1950s and 1960s hurricanes in the Miami area seem to be quite rare. Locating a view showing damage in Sunny Isles from 1960's Hurricane Donna was a major discovery. The Sunny Isle (no "s" on end) roof sign is shown here on top of a car in the motel's parking lot, following the storm. The driver of the Pontiac or Oldsmobile underneath the sign was probably not a happy camper!

The Sunny Isles Motel was sometimes the Sunny Isle Motel. This brochure and the one on the facing page clearly indicate the spelling difference.

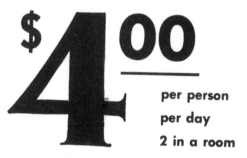

From Sandbar *to Sophistication*

A November 24, 1964 photograph depicts the Golden Gate, which put its name on the top of the building façade after taking over the Sun Ray motel property. However, in this photograph, the Sun Ray sign remains in place facing the south parking lot.

At 17601 Collins, the Sun Ranch was built in a Southwestern style. Note the flagstone facing the decorative wall to the right of the driveway, with the water wheel below the name of the motel.

MIAMI BEACH

SUN RANCH

RESORT MOTEL

at the Waterwheel (AAA) Approved

COMPLETELY AIR CONDITIONED
and HEATED

The brochure for the Sun Ranch provides an excellent close up of the sign, the facing wall and the water wheel.

MIAMI BEACH

Sun Village

RESORT · MOTEL

17400 COLLINS AVE.

FREE PARKING AT YOUR DOOR
ALL ROOMS STREET LEVEL

RATE SCHEDULE
JULY 1ST TO SEPTEMBER 5TH

$3.00

per person
per day
2 in a room

50 OF 150 ROOMS

GUARANTEED RATES
KITCHENETTES AVAILABLE

Sun Village was at 17400 Collins. At some point, the Sun Village was known as the Belmont Park. The rate shown on the Belmont Park flyer was four dollars per day, two in a room, while on this Sun Village brochure the rate has increased 50 percent to six dollars per day, two in a room!

Motel Row

The Tahiti was designed by Norman Giller and opened in 1951. The motel, at 16901 Collins, claimed to have a freshwater pool, which was unusual for the oceanfront hotels and motels, as it was so much less expensive simply to pump ocean water into the swimming pool.

Another Middle Eastern–themed property was the Tangiers, which opened in 1953 at 18695 Collins. Unlike many (if not most) of the inns along motel row, the Tangiers was not architecturally of note.

The Thunderbird was somewhat of a legend, even for Sunny Isles. The late and widely read columnist Walter Winchell mused, "In Miami Beach...the Thunderbird calls itself a motel...it is more like a palace." The brochure, shown here, covers every part of the motel and features the heated swimming pool on its cover.

Motel Row

This is a dramatic nighttime view of the motel. Note the massive decorative wall with the huge thunderbird in black, outlined with white lights facing the street.

Another view of the Thunderbird—this one in daylight and taken from the south drive looking north on December 9, 1955—gives an even closer perspective of the motel's namesake on the front facing wall. The motel was at 18601 Collins.

From Sandbar *to Sophistication*

At 15645 Collins, the Tony Sherman–designed Tropicana opened in 1951. The upper view presents the front of the building from the west side of Collins Avenue, the lower view shows the sun-worshipers catching the rays.

Motel Row

Waikiki was photographed on March 9, 1966, this view depicting the area north, on the east side of Collins. The motel opened in 1950 at 18801 Collins. A guest room interior shows the 1966 décor, complete with the then—de rigueur ashtray on the table at left.

Whispering Palms MOTEL

(AAA) OFFICIAL MOTEL

18901 COLLINS AVE.
MIAMI BEACH

100% AIR CONDITIONED

on the Ocean

MOTEL ROOMS

2.00

PER PERSON
Per Day

Double Occupancy

KITCHENETTES SLIGHTLY HIGHER

Beautiful and comfortably furnished rooms expressly designed for the new mode of casual, carefree motel living. All with Private Tub and Shower Bath.

How To Get There

DOWN U. S. 1, TURN LEFT DANIA, HOLLYWOOD, HALLANDALE, OR 163rd ST. TO A1A. **WHISPERING PALMS** RIGHT ON THE OCEAN AT 189th STREET.

Featuring . . .

- ★ Huge Private Beach
- ★ Tropical Patios
- ★ Free Beach Chairs Mats - Umbrellas
- ★ Free Parking
- ★ Shuffle Board
- ★ Coffee Shop
- ★ FREE ORANGE JUICE
- ★ TELEVISION and RADIOS
- ★ PRIVATE PHONES
- ★ Children Welcome

Present this folder at desk for these special rates

This flyer for four dollars per night, two in a room, must have been issued right after the Whispering Palms opened at 18901 Collins in 1953. Kitchenette rooms were priced slightly higher, and by this time each room had its own television.

Motel Row

The Windward was another of the initial 1950 properties. Located at 16051 Collins, it advertised an "Olympic swimming pool," but that, as we can see in this view, was pure hype. The said pool appears to be no more than 15 yards (45 feet) long, and an Olympic-sized pool is required to be at least 50 yards (150 feet) long.

In closing the motel era, we can see one of the inevitable occurrences that came with the motels: traffic jams! This view is looking south at 165th Street. The Atlantique docks (right) were across from the hotel, which was at 16501 Collins. The Sea Court, at 16200, is just a bit farther south on the right.

This photograph displays the two now-forgotten traffic circles at approximately 164th Street and directly across from the Santa Anita. The high-rises in the distant background were in Bal Harbour. Like the traffic photo on the previous page, this photo was taken on March 25 at the height of the 1959 winter tourist season.

Six

"The Times They Are A-Changin'"

From 1950 until the late 1980s, the hospitality industry, particularly the motel segment, was the heart and soul of Sunny Isles. However, as time went on, it became more and more evident that the owners of several of the inns were disinterested in making improvements and upgrading their properties. Many of the motels were not only falling into disrepair but were also attracting a less than desirable element, with calls for police assistance increasing regularly.

Fortunately, Raanan Katz moved to the area from Boston, where he had acquired and developed retail properties. In 1985 he began buying and redeveloping existing shopping centers in Sunny Isles, upgrading and improving them.

Meanwhile, a number of private individuals, headed by the Concerned Citizens of Northeast Dade County, were acutely aware of not only the deteriorating conditions of the motels but also of the paucity of services being extended to Sunny Isles by the county. For example, the nearest police station was on Biscayne Boulevard in North Miami Beach and response times averaged close to fifteen minutes.

With the community agitating for major improvements in government services, a small group began meeting on a regular basis to determine what actions would best serve the people of Sunny Isles. On April 12, 1996, Irving Turetsky, David Samson, Norman S. Edelcup, Danny Iglesias and Irving Diamond met with attorney Gene Sterns to start incorporation proceedings. On January 7, 1997, 2,678 (a huge 72 percent) of the registered voters in Sunny Isles cast "yes" ballots for incorporation.

On February 1 of that year, State Senator Gwen Margolis appointed a charter commission, consisting of Robert J. Lilienfeld (chairperson), Roslyn P. Brezin, Emanuel Lassar, Judge Manuel Ramos and W. Donald Stewart. Lynn M. Dannheiser served as attorney to the commission, and on April 4 the city charter was completed, signed and dated. On June 16, the charter was adopted.

On July 29, 1997, the first city commission—consisting of David P. Samson as mayor and commissioners Irving Turetsky, Danny Iglesias, Lila Kauffman and Connie Morrow—was elected.

The hiring of appropriate city officials began. On March 1, 1998, the first city hall opened, located in the 170th Street R.K. shopping center. At the end of that month, the city's police department came into existence and Sunny Isles Beach police began patrolling their own seven-month-old city. On October 5, the first city budget, which included

"The Times They Are A-Changin'"

property tax as city revenue, was adopted. A little over a month later, the city received its first property tax revenue check.

The year 2001 would begin with a joyful celebration, as the city's first new hotel or motel in thirty years—the Ocean Point, built by J. Milton and Associates—would open its doors. The following year, on October 29, 2002, ground was broken for the new city hall complex at 18070 Collins Avenue, on the west side of the street.

Sadly, October 12, 2003, would be a day of mourning and reflection for the city, as David P. Samson, one of its founding fathers—and the first mayor—died. Three months later, on January 8, 2004, Norman S. Edelcup became mayor of the city he loved, a position he continues to hold in 2007. Mayor Edelcup is respected by the entire community for his forthrightness, honesty and total integrity in dealing with the business and affairs of the great city he helped to create. His total devotion to the city was also reflected by his involvement in the initial incorporation proceedings and his 2003 election to the city commission as vice-mayor.

The city's official seal, which was created by Charles Wachsberg, is simple yet elegant. It reflects the tropical beauty that the city's visionary founders—along with its current commission and administration—foresaw and currently see as a major part and benefit of the community. Along with a stunning new look, Sunny Isles Beach offers residents and visitors opportunities for the use of beaches and parks that were previously unavailable or non-existent.

From Sandbar *to Sophistication*

Sunny Isles Beach's past is exemplified by the original Harvey B. Graves–built bridges, which have been declared historic sites by the city. The photograph of the beautiful Atlantic Isle Lagoon bridge was taken in March 2006 by Richard C. Schulman.

"The Times They Are A-Changin'"

OFFICIAL GUIDE
MIAMI BEACH
OCEANFRONT MOTELS

1975/1976 Winter/Spring Rates
AREA MAP • THINGS TO SEE & DO

4000 ROOMS – 34 MOTELS
ALL MEMBERS OF THE
GREATER MIAMI BEACH MOTEL ASSOCIATION
PLEDGED TO THE
"CODE OF ETHICS"
YOU CAN RESERVE WITH CONFIDENCE

Winter 1976

WHEN CHECKING-IN
ASK FOR YOUR
FREE GIFT

SUNNYISLESBEACH
F L O R I D A
HOTEL & MOTEL DIRECTORY

Just North of Miami Beach.
A World of Vacation Fun!

The Miami Beach Motel Association encompassed Sunny Isles but not Miami Beach, using the Miami Beach name for national recognition, even though Sunny Isles is close to five miles north of the Miami Beach city limits. The 1975–76 season brochure for the association is shown here with the circa 1996–97 brochure published by the renamed Sunny Isles Beach Resort Association. At the time of publication, the association included twenty-four motels totaling 3,700 rooms, indicating that a number of the smaller motels had been bought by developers and were no longer extant. *Courtesy Rose Rice.*

Looking west from the Sunny Isles Beach historical landmark Sunny Isles–Newport Pier, the old is juxtapositioned with the new. The pier provides a wonderful foreground to the Oceania buildings, just south of 167th Street, on the site of the old Castaways.

The 1967-built Newport is in the foreground, with the brand-new Sands Point building at 16711 Collins Avenue behind it. *Photograph by Richard C. Schulman.*

The new city has made it a point to become flora-friendly. In addition to new parks, the mayor, commission and city manager have urged both businesses and citizens to "plant," a charge that has been taken seriously. Even though the Driftwood Motel is no longer in existence, the owners did their part at 17121 Collins—prior to the sale of the property—to landscape and enhance the appearance of the 1952 structure. *Courtesy Rose Rice.*

Beautifying and enhancing the city, Raanan Katz has, at all of his R.K. shopping centers, made a determined effort to plant more trees and increase green space. At 16850 Collins is R.K. Town Center, and this Richard C. Schulman photograph is indicative of Mr. Katz's dedication to the city.

"The Times They Are A-Changin'"

The longtime Wolfie Cohen's Rascal House sign was always looked for by motorists anxious to read the latest phrase.

From Sandbar *to Sophistication*

Wolfie Cohen is but a memory but the new "rascals" who now preside over the Rascal House are (left to right) Ike and Jason Starkman who, in addition to having bought the Rascal House, have purchased Miami Beach's famous Epicure Market.

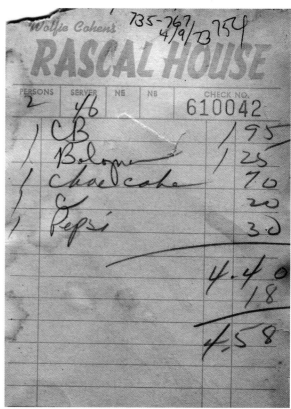

On April 9, 1973, the author and a date enjoyed an evening snack at the Rascal. The check total, including $1.95 for a corned beef sandwich, was $4.58 including tax.

"The Times They Are A-Changin'"

PAMELL 7384 Ck#1 Gs 3 10/13/06 13:22
======== Order# **745281** =======0928

****
******** G U E S T Receipt *********
****
 Iced Tea   1.85
 NO BEVERAGE
 Clam Chowder Cup   4.75
 Tuna Salad Halfer   7.35
     Tomatoes (50)
 Tuna Salad Halfer   6.85
           Subtotal   20.80
           Tax   1.66
              TOTAL   22.46

 CASH   23.00-

Cash CHANGE   .54

        WE APPRECIATE
        YOUR BUSINESS
     CATERING & TAKE OUT
       (305) 947-4581

On October 13, 2006, the author had lunch with friends from Sunny Isles Beach; the check, including two half tuna salad sandwiches was $22.46. Indeed, "the times, they are a-changin'!"

From Sandbar *to Sophistication*

On September 28, 2006, the Historical Association of Southern Florida inaugurated their six-month-long "Miami Beach: A Tropical Paradise" exhibit with a gala party and contributor's introduction event. Sunny Isles Beach, which was a major part of the exhibit, graciously loaned a great piece of history and a wonderful memory—the Driftwood Motel pelican—to the museum. The old—the pelican—is shown with the new—Sunny Isles Beach Vice-Mayor Roslyn P. Brezin (left) and Mayor Norman S. Edelcup (right). *Photograph by Richard C. Schulman.*

"The Times They Are A-Changin'"

That same night, Mayor Edelcup (far left) and Vice-Mayor Brezin (far right) were joined by (center from left) Marilyn Gleason, widow of Jackie Gleason, and Commissioner Lewis J. Thaler, standing behind Mrs. Thaler. *Photograph by Richard C. Schulman.*

There is something bittersweet about saying goodbye to an old friend, but the old order must change to make way for the new. The Trump Royale, a project of the Dezer-Trump-Dezer partnership, towers over the Suez Oceanfront Resort sign at 182nd and Collins.

From Sandbar *to Sophistication*

The coming of the new era is nowhere more poignantly shown than in this photograph. Sad as it may be to see the fallen Suez Motel sign in front of the stunning new Trump Royale, the Royale is the herald of a glorious new era for Sunny Isles Beach. When the lights go out in finality, those buildings that can no longer stand the test of time must enter the darkest of nights into which, at the end of day, all things eventually must go.

Seven

Taking Sunny Isles Beach into the Future

There is an excitement within this ten-year-old city that is rarely—if ever—found in municipalities these days. Something great and incredible has transformed Sunny Isles Beach from a strip of mostly run-down, not-aging-well motels to a jazzy, electrifying, luminescent place, with a demographic that most localities would give their eyeteeth for!

A progressive, caring administration has done something no other city in the county—and possibly in the state—has ever done: it appointed, less than ten years after its founding, a city historian whose task is to preserve both photographs and artifacts of the city's past. The History Hall in City Hall is a source of pride for every city employee and resident. But the city fathers have done much more—naming four sites as historic landmarks, cajoling developers to donate or sell space for municipal parks, opening beachfront access where there was none before, providing free shuttle service for residents, honoring Holocaust survivors and donating $10 million to the Miami-Dade County School District toward the cost of construction of a Sunny Isles Beach K-8 public school, the first ever for the city or its unincorporated predecessor.

The federal government, heeding the worthwhile requests of the city administration, opened a U.S. post office on the first floor of city hall. The county, knowing the great emphasis that the citizens of Sunny Isles Beach place on reading and learning, has opened a branch public library. Sunny Isles Beach today is, simply put, the hottest spot in Greater Miami for new businesses to open and for people to live.

What most non-residents are not aware of is that this incredible city is not just an avenue of high-rises that supplanted the motels; rather, it is a work in progress, with ongoing plans for cultural events, community activities and citizen involvement. Perhaps best of all is that there are two areas of the city reserved for single-family homes, the property values of which have increased unceasingly, especially since incorporation in 1997.

In 2007 the city will celebrate its tenth anniversary and that event will be part of a series of milestone activities that will do nothing but add to the aura of Sunny Isles Beach. It is one of the finest places in America in which to live, work, raise children and enjoy life. With the continued leadership of Mayor Edelcup and the current commission, the city can only continue its march toward the absolute pinnacle of quality in government, services, opportunities for residents and investors and—most of all—its caring attitude about its past, present and future.

From Sandbar *to Sophistication*

Sunny Isles Beach's first mayor, David P. Samson served from July 29, 1997, until his death on October 12, 2003.

Taking Sunny Isles Beach into the Future

The city's second and current mayor, its biggest booster and the driving force behind so many of the great and exciting things happening in Sunny Isles Beach is Norman S. Edelcup.

The current city commission includes (from left) Lewis J. Thaler, Gerry Goodman, Mayor Edelcup, Vice-Mayor Roslyn P. Brezin and Danny Iglesias.

City Manager John Szerlag

Director of Administrative Services Alyce Hanson

City Attorney Hans Ottinot

City Clerk Jane A. Hines

Taking Sunny Isles Beach into the Future

Fred Maas is the city's highly regarded chief of police, responsible for a sixty-five-person department, including an ATV unit, motorcycles, a canine unit, patrol officers, detectives, a bicycle unit, a crime scene unit, marine patrol and administrative services.

Richard C. Schulman is city historian, as well as administrative aide to the mayor and commission.

The police motorcycle unit consists of (from left) Officers Yojan Martinez and Stephen Brenton, Acting Sergeant Kenny Hackett and Officers Steve Hamedl and Javier Estevez.

Taking Sunny Isles Beach into the Future

Guarding Sunny Isles Beach's waterways and the Atlantic, the marine patrol includes Sergeant Bobby Randazzo (left) and Detective Blake Royal.

Using all-terrain vehicles (ATVs), Officer Melissa Montesino and Sergeant Lee Athanasiou help to ensure the safety of the city's beachgoers.

The beautiful La Perla, directly south of the Newport, is a Kobi Karp, AIA, creation. The city's waterways and beaches are evident in this photo, and visitors and residents are made to feel secure by a superb police department that gives Sunny Isles one of the lowest crime rates in the nation.

It is a very special community that seeks out and memorializes the living survivors of the Holocaust and honors the three hundred survivors of that horrific tragedy living in Sunny Isles Beach. It is obvious that the dedication to creating a marvelous and exciting lifestyle goes hand in hand—at least in Sunny Isles Beach—with honoring the survivors of the most terrible event in human history.

Blessing for Life

בָּרוּךְ אַתָּה יְיָ, אֱלֹהֵינוּ מֶלֶךְ הָעוֹלָם, שֶׁהֶחֱיָנוּ וְקִיְּמָנוּ וְהִגִּיעָנוּ לַזְּמַן הַזֶּה.

Praised be Thou, O Lord our God, King of the universe who kept us in life, and sustained us and enabled us to reach this season.

"Survivors of the Holocaust"
Sunny Isles Beach, Florida • Temple B'nai Zion
Sunday, March 28, 2004 • 1:30 p.m.

Taking Sunny Isles Beach into the Future

The Lehman Causeway, connecting Aventura with Sunny Isles Beach at 192nd Street, is named for Congressman William "Bill" Lehman, who, through his work on various congressional committees, always fought for south Florida's residents. The causeway was dedicated to him for his efforts in facilitating its construction. Shown here on the steps of the Capitol with three of his constituents, the congressman was known for his warmth and graciousness.

With the renaissance of Sunny Isles Beach, the sandy beach has become accessible to all, not just the guests of the motels. Here a group enjoys a game of volleyball with several of the magnificent new condos in the background.

The causeway is clearly shown in this photograph, which includes the R.K. Aventura Beach Plaza at 18090–18290 Collins Avenue. The private homes of the Golden Shores section of the city are behind and to the right of the shopping center, and the towers of Aventura stretch from left to right. *Courtesy R.K. Centers.*

From Sandbar *to Sophistication*

The influence of Kobi Karp, AIA, and his architectural firm on reshaping the look and feel of Sunny Isles Beach has been nothing short of extraordinary. His bold new designs and glamorous concepts have the same effect on Sunny Isles Beach that Morris Lapidus had on Miami Beach in its greatest hotel days. The Sole is a striking example of Karp's work.

Taking Sunny Isles Beach into the Future

Kobi Karp's Sunny Isles Beach Marina is a triumph of shapes and sizing, the building being close to perfect in both its setting and design. Note the unusual use of concrete in setting off the terraces.

The Trump Grande, at right, is nothing short of stunning. From the partnership of Dezer-Trump-Dezer, the building is another of the beautiful and momentous structures that have made both the Dezers and Donald Trump famous.

Gil Dezer (left), with his University of Miami degree in international finance and marketing, in association with his father, Michael (right) and Donald Trump have brought a new level of elegance and quality to Sunny Isles Beach. Superb hoteliers and builders, the Dezers are now the largest oceanfront property owners in the city with over twenty-seven acres of prime oceanfront in their portfolio.

As America's bold new city of the future moves inexorably toward its destiny as Florida's Riviera, its greatness in metamorphosing from a weary resort town to a magnificent residential and destination community is most clearly shown by its appreciation for, and willingness to honor, its past. As a fitting tribute to its history, the city has preserved—and placed on display in Senator Gwen Margolis Park—the Colonial Inn horses and carriage. *Photograph by Richard C. Schulman.*

Taking Sunny Isles Beach into the Future

The city has dedicated the futuristic statue of *The Family* by Sunny Isles resident and artist David Fisher to a new generation, placing it in Samson Oceanfront Park. The great city of Sunny Isles Beach, with its strong leadership, dedication to both its past and its future and a belief in itself and its people, has become one of the nation's greatest municipal and government success stories. *Photograph by Richard C. Schulman.*

Visit us at
www.historypress.net